PRINCIPLE OF BUSINESS FINANCE

FOR BEGINNERS

Wale Ogunsola is a graduate of the Accounting, a professional Accountant, professional manager, MBA in business administration and holds BSC in political science and international relations.

He is an entrepreneur with interest in the hospitality and real estate business.

He is also a writer with keen interest in entrepreneurship, business, and political books.

He has the following books to his credit: fundamentals of accounting, how get started and earn through amazon KDP, Freelance and Affiliate marketing for beginners, The silence of the president among others

Some of these books are available on amazon, other bookshelves, and local markets.

About the Book

This book contains everything you need to know about finance for beginners.

Principle of Business finance for beginners is essentially prepared for students of finance, candidates preparing for finance related examinations. In addition, the book will be useful for practicing businessmen, financial mangers and those who wish to develop themselves in business finance: as no previous knowledge of the course is assumed in its preparation.

In the book, essential principles of finance are used to make laudable financial decisions that can contribute towards the development of business organization. Not by rule of thumb used by financial managers, which had led to poor decisions and costly mistakes leading to many business failures.

The book has been structured in such a way that will aid easy understanding of users.

Forward

This book is not just for beginners, its for those need deep search for financial knowledge and the rudiment of business functions.

Many businesses are finding it extremely difficult to survive the business not only because of the business environment and pollical and economic factor but also due to deficient knowledge of business accounting and finances.

There is no doubt the author had brought to bear his wealth of experience to writing this book.

Business finance is beginners is 100% value for money.

Yemi Balogun (MBA)

© Copyright 2021 by Wale Ogunsola

This book may not be copied or reprinted for commercial use or profit. It cannot be shared, distributed, or reproduced, except by or with the permission of the author.

Contents

About the Author

About the book

Forward

NATURE OF FINANCE..8

SOURCES AND APPLICATION OF FUNDS....................33

CAPITAL FORMATION:..82

MANAGEMENT OF FINANCIAL RESOURCE...............106

NATURE OF FINANCE

Finance is the science of raising funds to organize, reorganize or extend an enterprise. It is the process of sourcing and managing of funds to achieve the organizational goals and objectives. Finance is the provision of money when and where needed, that is, it involves the acquisition and use of funds.

Business relates to commercial activities put together to enhance wealth maximization. It entails buying and selling i.e. trade. Business generally face the fundamental problems of "what investments to make" and how to pay for them".

TYPES OF BUSINESS:

Business can be grouped into: Sole Proprietorship, Partnership and Corporation/Public Company.

Sole Proprietorship

The sole proprietorship is a business which is owned by one person who operates it for his own profit. In essence, the sole proprietor is self-employed. The typical sole proprietorship is a small firm, such as "Cement Stores", "Provision Kiosk", Auto repair shop or shoe repair business. Most often the proprietor, along with a few employees (who may be members of his family) operate the proprietorship. Sole proprietorship occurs where one starts a business on his own without partner. He bears all the costs and keeps all the profits after tax. He has unlimited liability. That is, his personal property can be sold to pay the business debt in case of default.

Other characteristics of sole proprietorship are:

1. The financial and other risks associated with the business are all borne by the sole owner.

2. The owner shoulders the entire responsibility for the management and operation of the business.

3. The capital of the business is provided by the owner, though to make a start he may have to borrow from friends or relations.

The majority of the sole proprietorship business in Nigeria are in the wholesale, retail or service industries.

Advantages of a Sole Proprietorship

The commonly cited advantages of a sole proprietorship aside from being one's own boss, are as follows.

1. It is easily and inexpensively formed that is, no formal procedure of operation is required and it is subject to only a few government regulations.

2. Self interest is a powerful motive making for the success of the one man business. He has every incentive to make his business as efficient as possible. He is in full charge and

can devote as much of his time and energy to it as he wishes.

3. Self-independence: There is freedom of taking any action or decision in this type of business.

4. The business pays no corporate income taxes, rather; all earnings are subject to personal income taxes.

5. Ownership of all profits goes to the sole proprietor. Many people do not like the idea of working for someone else and being exploited by their employer. The sole proprietorship allows the owner to receive the fruits of his effort.

Disadvantages of a Sole Proprietorship

The following are some of the disadvantages of Sole proprietorship business:

1. The smallness of the capital may hinder expansion.

2. The business usually dies as a result of the death of the proprietor. No continuity. The personal abilities of the sole proprietor determines the success of the business, and on his death or retirement, continued success depends on the ability of the person who inherits the business, but there is no assurance that his successor will possesses the required ability.

3. Unlimited liability: The sole proprietor bears all the risk of the business and thus personally liable for all the debts and obligations of the firm. He cannot, for

example, limit his liability to the capital he has invested in the business.

4. Cannot obtain the benefits of Economics of scale. This type of business is unsuitable for any form of production where economics of scale are available.

5. High labour turnover: This type of business lacks necessary motivation to retain workers for a long period. Hence, the employees always look for better offer in well organized institutions. Therefore, sole proprietorship usually lacks experienced and highly skilled workers.

Partnership

Partnership occurs when two or more people or business associates pool resources together to form a business. A partnership agreement is formed which stipulates how management decisions are to be made and the proportion of profits and loses to which each partner is entitled, provisions for salaries and the procedure to be followed if a partner withdraws from the business or firm is dissolved. The partners then pay personal income tax on their share of profits. Partners have unlimited liability except in larger businesses where "general" and "limited" partners exit.

Limited Partnership

The most common of the special types of partnership is the limited partnership. In a general, or regular partnership all the parties have unlimited liabilities; that is, their personal assets can be claimed when the firm defaults on its obligations. In a limited partnership, one or more partners can be designated as having limited liability as long as, at least, one partner has unlimited liability. The limited partner is normally prohibited from being active in the management of the firm. The advantage of limited partnership is that an individual can invest money and expect a return without assuming any liability beyond the amount of his investment.

Advantages of Partnership

1. High capital: The financial resources of more than one person provides higher amount of capital.

2. Easy formation: Like the sole proprietorship, it is easy and economical to establish.

3. Less control: There is a very limited amount of governmental control.

4. More articulate decision-making process. There is the benefit of combined judgement as more sensible heads better than one.

Disadvantages of Partnership

1. Short life span: When a particular dies or withdraws from the business, the partnership is dissolved.

2. Unlimited liability: Each of the general partners is liable for the partnerships debt. That is, has unlimited personal liability for the business's debts.

3. Problem of investment withdrawal. It is difficult for a partner to liquidate or transfer money invested in the partnership.

4. Limited scale: Although the partnership business can grow larger than a sole proprietorship, still, it has difficulty in growing to large-scale operations.

Corporations

According to Justice Marshall, a former Chief Justice of the United States of America, a corporation is "an artificial being, invisible, intangible and existing only in the contemplation of the law". This type of business is a legal entity distinct from its owners and managers.

Corporation is a legal entity that can sue and be sued. It is taxed separately. Corporations have limited liability. One distinct feature of corporations is the separation of ownership and management which gives them more flexibility and permanence than Partnership and Proprietorship where the owners are the managers.

Corporations become Public Companies when its shares are quoted and traded on Stock Exchange.

Characteristics of a Corporation

1. Legal entity: It is legal entity separate from its owners that is, may sue and be sued by another person including the owner.

2. It is always based on law or Charter, which states the purpose of a corporation and the general limitation within the firm may operate.

3. Unlimited life-span: It has an unlimited life, though ownership composition may continue to change.

4. Ownership belongs to shareholders and can be transferred without the necessity of obtaining permission from other shareholders.

5. It is subject to a variety of taxes.

6. The corporate officers are responsible for the day-to-day operations of the firm.

7. The Board of Directors is responsible for directing the affairs of the business and final authority rests with them.

Advantages of a Corporation

1. Limited liability: The liability of the shareholder is limited to the fully paid-up value of the shares he holds so that if the company should find itself in difficulties and unable to meet the financial obligations to its creditors the shareholder can lose no more than the amount he has invested in the business.

2. Opportunity to raise more capital: Since the maximum possible loss is known in advance, shares are readily marketable and capital can be raised from many individuals

through the sale of stock (shares and debentures).

3. Share Transfer: Transfer of ownership can easily be effected through organized stock exchange.

4. Benefit of Continuity: The company has perpetual life span. The death or withdrawal of an owner does not liquidate the company.

Disadvantages of Corporation

1. Cost: The expenses incurred in the process of incorporation are very large.

2. Statutory requirements: Due to the fact that corporation is a legal entity, it is subject to regulation by various state and Federal government departments and Agencies, Often, returns and other information are

required in order to fulfil the requirements of these regulatory agencies.

Others. Other demerits of corporation include the lack of personal interest in the firm by employees due to their often-non-owner status and a lack of secrecy, since each shareholder must be provided with an annual report of the corporation's financial position.

Business finance means sourcing and using of funds for business activities. It is therefore the responsibility of financial manager to plan for, forecast, obtain, and use funds to maximize the value of a firm. Hence, the functions of a financial manager include financial analysis and planning, the management of the firm's asset structure and financial structure.

Relationship of Finance to various Departments of an Organization

Finance serves as a pivot upon which other departments revolve, other departments prepare budgets to execute their objectives. It is the finance department that plans, co-ordinates and controls the finance to enable other departments function well.

Departments like Sales, Purchasing, Marketing, Production, Personnel and others cannot operate successfully without finance. For instance, recruitment and promotion of employees in all departments require payment of wages and salaries and other benefits, and thus, involves finance. In the same vein, buying a new machine or replacing an old one for the purpose of increasing productive capacity affects the use of funds. Sales promotion, advertising and other marketing activities require use of cash and, therefore, affect financial resources. Almost all kinds of business activities directly or indirectly involve the acquisition and the use of money.

Finance department therefore serves other departments to enhance the corporate objectives by harmonizing their functions.

Contributions of Business Finance to the overall growth of an organization

The contribution of Business Finance to the overall growth of an organization can be well appreciated through its functions discussed as follows:

Efficient acquisition and using of funds for profit: Through its financing decision, the business finance or financial manager ensures that capital funds are raised from reliable and cost-efficient sources and are used efficiently for generating returns and paying returns to the suppliers of funds. It also determines the financial structure of the firm.

Investment function: Business finance takes care of the total investment in a company. It determines the quantity and quality of the assets, its cost, and business risks involved and expected returns on assets employed.

Capital gain through entity: The financial manager determines whether his company should source funds from money or capital market or both depending on the duration and cost. He ensures that the market price of his company's shares appreciates enough for the company's shareholders to realize capital gain through entity. Capital gain occurs when there is increase in the value of shares, which can enhance profit from the sale of such shares.

Dividend decision is another vital function of business finance. It determines the percentage or amount of firm's earning to be paid to shareholders as dividends in order to maximize their wealth and satisfy the contributors of capital (satisfying). It also determines the retained earnings to plough back into the business. In essence, the business finance strikes the balance between the risk and profitability i.e. risk-return trade off.

Inflation: The business finance tries to minimize the effect of inflation, interest and exchange rates on the firm's performance. In as much as inflation distorts profits, lenders avoid longer-term fixed rate loans in favour of variable rate loans where their return is responsive to changes in inflation.

Asset Structure: The financial manager determines both the mix and the types assets found on the firm's balance sheet. The mix refers to the number of Naira of current and fixed assets. Once the mix is determined, the financial manager must determine and attempt to maintain certain "optimal" levels of each type of current asset. He must also determine which are the best fixed assets to acquire. He must know when existing fixed assets become obsolete and need to be replaced or modified. The determination of the best asset structure for the firm is not a simple process; it require insight into the past and future operations of the firm and an understanding of its long-run objectives.

Use of Money Capital Market: The financial manager is the anchor person that links his firm to the financial markets in which funds are raised and in which the firm's securities are traded.

Financial Information Analysis: The financial manager's main function here is to transform the financial data into a form that can be used to monitor the firm's financial position, to plan for future financing, to evaluate the need for increased productivity, and to determine what additional financing is required. It is pertinent that this function must be performed properly in order to enable the financial manager execute his other key functions of determining the firm's asset and financial venture.

Employee welfare: Through business finance adequate attention is paid to the welfare of employee in terms of wages, salaries, recreation, health facilities and other incentives.

Creditors: It is the responsibility of the business finance to ensure that financial obligations are met when due to avoid the ugly situation of company liquidation.

Social responsibility: Business finance strives for company's viability by making provision for the welfare of all stakeholders in the company. Effort are made to ensure clean environment devoid of air and water pollution. There is also provision for basic amenities like schools, good roads, potable water and health facilities for neighbouring communities.

Customer satisfaction: Business Finance ensures the growth of the company by improving the standard, quality and adequate value for money spent on the goods or services produced. It works for customer satisfaction and increasing patronage.

The above analyzed functions in effect, affect the size, growth, profitability and risk of the firm and ultimately, the value of the firm.

SOURCES AND APPLICATION OF FUNDS

Sources of finance indicate how a business organization generates its funds or forms of financing a business to achieve its objectives. Funds are required for the attainment of the Business organization's goals and objectives. It is needed for day-to-day activities, rehabilitation, expansion, take-off, growth, and survival of any organization, whether entrepreneur, partnership, private and public limited liability companies, or joint stock ventures.

Things to consider before borrowing:

Sources – The sources of finance should be well defined. It should be determined whether to use internal or external funds, debt or owner's funds, long term, or short-term financing, for the project to be executed.

Risk – The risk of the project to be financed should be considered whether it would be self financing or not.

Duration of the project should also be considered. It is financial suicidal to obtain short term loan for a long-term project.

Cost – Cost of finance should be considered in relation to the type of the project and its proceeds.

Restrictions and Regulations – The borrower and lender should examine the or otherwise of the loan agreement and nature of the project.

Types of Funds

Basically, there are three sources of finance

Short term – This finance is available from a month to a year.

Medium term – The fund can be utilized from year to five years.

Long term – This fund is usually sourced for capital projects. The duration of the loan is five years and above.

Short Term Funds

These are funds repayable within one year. Short term fund should not be used to finance long term project/Asset to avoid bankruptcy or insolvency.

Types of Short Term Funds:

i. Bank Overdraft – This is an advance granted by bank to its customers on interest. It may be secured or not but payable on demand.

Advantages:

- Bank overdraft is not expensive

- It requires low interest charges

- It is easy to process

- It usually requires no collateral

Disadvantages:

- Unsecured, this makes default imminent

- It is given on prohibitive condition. For instance, the money can be called without notice.

- Only the bank's customers are entitled to it.

ii. Trade Credits / Account Payable

Trade credit is a short term finance that a customer gets from the supplier of goods in the normal course of business. Trade credits involve no costs if there is no cash discount or if the amount is paid within the discount period, otherwise there will be cost incurred. The implicit or defective cost of not taking a discount is written thus:

Percentage of discount   x 360

100% of discount   Maximum payment period-period discount

Trade credits usually involve terms of credit.

Credit Terms: The terms of credit specify the period for which credit is extended and the discount if any given for early payment. For instance, terms of credit may allow 2% discount if payment is made within 10 days and the entire amount is due 30 days from the invoice date if the discount is not taken.

This is normally written as "2/10 net 30 EOM" / 'MOM".

If the terms are stated as 'net within 60 days' this indicates that no discount is offered and that the invoice is due and payable 60 days after the invoice date.

The firm's credit terms state the credit period, the size of the cash discount, the cash discount period, and the date the credit begins. Each of these aspects of a firm's credit terms is concisely stated in such expressions as stated above. That is, "2/10 net 30 E.O.M". These terms contain all the key information concerning the length of the credit period (30 days), the cash discount (2 percent), the cash discount period (10 days), and the time the credit period begins (the end of the month). Although credit terms typically differ among industries, there are number of commonly used terms each of which is discussed briefly below.

The credit period: The credit period is the number of days until payment in full is required. Regardless of whether a cash discount is offered, the credit period associated with a transaction must be indicated. Credit periods usually range from zero to 120 days, although in certain instances longer credit period is provided.

The net period: Most credit terms include a net period, which is typically referred to as "net 30 days", "net 60 days" and so on. The prefix net indicates that the face amount of the purchase must be paid within the number of days indicated form the beginning of the credit period.

Cash discounts: The cash discount is a percentage deduction from the purchase price allowed the purchaser if he pays within the cash discount period. A 2 percent cash discount indicates that the purchaser of N100 of merchandise need pay only N98 if he pays within the discount period.

From the point of view of the supplier of credit, whose objective is to collect his accounts receivable quickly, a cash discount provides incentive for the purchaser to pay early. The reduction in proceeds due to the discount is compensated for by the speeding up of collections. The purchaser, whose objective is to stretch is accounts payable by paying as late as possible, must determine whether it is advantageous for him to take the cash discount and pay early.

The cash discount period. This specifies the maximum number of days after the beginning of the credit period that the cash discount can be taken. Typically, the cash discount period is between 5 and 20 days. In certain industries more than one discount is offered. The discount period is shortest for largest discount offered and longest for the smallest discount offered.

The beginning of the credit period. This is stated as part of the supplier's credit terms. It can be specified in various way – as the date of the invoice, the end of the month and the middle of the month.

The notation "E.O.M" (end of the month) indicates that the credit period for all purchases made within a given month begins on the first of the month immediately following. The date of the invoice is recognized as the date of sale.

The notation "M.O.M" (middle of the month) indicates that the month is broken into two separate credit periods. The credit period for all sales made (i.e., invoices dated) between the first and fifteenth of the month begins on the 16th of the month. The credit period for all sales made between the sixteenth and the thirtieth of the month begins on the first day of the month immediately following.

The cost of trade credit: Although no explicit cost is levied on the recipient of trade credit, the firm extending the credit does incur a cost in the sense that its money is tied up for the interim. Extending credit to customers requires the investment of money that could be used elsewhere, and this cost is indirectly passed on the purchaser in the cost of the merchandise.

Foregoing the cash discount: If a firm is extended credit terms which include a cash discount, it has two options. Its first option is to take the cash discount. Taking the cash discount will require the firm to pay earlier than it would have to if the discount were foregone. In many instances firms take the cash discount regardless of whether payment is made within the cash discount period. If a firm does intend to take a cash discount, it should pay on the last day of the cash discount period.

The second option open to the firm is to forgo the cash discount and pay at the end of the credit period. Although there is no direct cost associated with foregoing a cash discount, there is an implicit cost. If the cash discount is foregone, the firm should pay on the final day of the credit period. A firm should pay its bills as late as it can without damaging its credit rating. We shall assume that if a discount is foregone payment will be made on the final day of the credit period.

Illustration: -

The TAKAS company purchased N1,000 worth of merchandise on February 27 from a supplier extending terms of 2/10 net 30 E.O.M if the corporation takes the cash discount, it will have to pay N980 (N1,000 – 0.02 (N1,000) on March 10. If it foregoes the discount, it will have to pay the full N1,000 on March 30.

The cost of foregoing a cash discount: -

There is an implicit cost in foregoing a cash discount. This is because to delay paying its bill for an additional number of days, the firm must forego an opportunity to pay less for the items it has purchased. The cost of foregoing a cash discount can be illustrated by a simple example. The example below assumes that if the firm takes a cash discount, payment will be made on the final day of the cash discount period and if the cash discount is foregone payment will be made on the final day of the credit period.

Illustration:-

The TAKAS Company, mentioned in the proceeding example, has been extended credit terms of 2/10 net 30 E.O.M. If it takes the cash discount on its February 27 purchase, payment will be required on March 10. If the cash discount is foregone, payment can be made on March 30. In order to keep its money (i.e. postpone payment) for an extra 20 days (from March 10 to March 30) the firm must forego an opportunity to pay N980 for its N1,000 purchase. In other words, it will cost the firm an extra N20 to delay payment for 20 days.

To calculate the cost of foregoing the cash discount, the true purchase price must be viewed as the discounted cost of the merchandise. For the TAKAS Company, this discounted cost will be N980. In order to avoid paying the N980 for an extra 20 days, the firm must pay N20 (N1,000 –

N980). The annual percentage cost of foregoing the cash discount can be calculated using the example.

Cost of foregoing cash discount = $\dfrac{CD}{1-CD} \times \dfrac{360}{N}$

Where

CD = the stated cash discount in percentage terms

N = the number of days payment can be delayed by foregoing the cash discount.

Substitute the value for

CD = .02 and N = 20 days into the above equation

Cost of foregoing cash discount = $\dfrac{.02}{.98} \times \dfrac{360}{20}$

= 36.73%

The same answer can be obtained by using the equation:

Cost of foregoing cash discount = $\dfrac{CD}{CP-DP} \times \dfrac{360}{1}$

Where

CD = cash discount

CP = credit period

DP = discount period

Substituting the value from the last illustration

Cost of foregoing cash discount = 2% X 360
30-10   1

Using the cost of foregoing a cash discount in decision making: -

The financial manager must determine whether it is advisable to take a cash discount. There are also a few other decisions with respect to cash discounts that may confront the financial manager. Each of these decisions can be illustrated by a simple example.

Illustration: -

The Tee and Tee Company has four possible suppliers, each offering different credit terms. Except for the differences in credit terms, their products and services are undifferentiated. The table below presents the credits terms offered by each supplier, A, B, C, and D and the cost of foregoing the cash discounts. The approximate method of calculating the cost of foregoing a cash discount has been used in order to simplify the analysis. The cost of foregoing the cash discount from the four suppliers are as shown in the table below:-

Cash discounts and associated costs for the Tee and Tee Company

Supplier Credit terms Approximate cost of foregoing cash discount

A 2/10 net 30 EOM 36%

B 1/10 net 70 EOM 6%

C 3/20 net 60 EOM 27%

D 4/10 net 60 EOM 28.7%

Let us now see how the above information might be used.

Case 1: If the firm needs short term funds, which are currently available from its commercial bank at 12 percent, and if each of the suppliers (A,B,C and D) are viewed separately, which (if any) of the suppliers' cash discount fill the firm forego?

In order to answer the question, each suppliers' term must be evaluated as they would be if it were the firm's sole supplier. A decision can then be made based on the consequences of the stated credit terms: -

Supplier A: the firm will take the cash discount since the cost of foregoing is 36 percent. The firm will then borrow the fund it requires from its commercial bank at 12 percent interest.

Supplier B: the firm will do better to forego the cash discount since the cost of this action is less than the cost of borrowing money from the bank (6 percent as opposed to 12 percent).

Supplier C: the firm should take the cash discount since in both cases the cost of foregoing the discounts is greater than the 12 percent cost of borrowing from the bank.

Case 2: If the Tee and Tee Company knows that it must forego cash discounts since it needs money and has no alternative sources of short term financing, from which of its four alternative suppliers will the purchase be made?

In this case, the main concern is not with the cost of foregoing the cash discount, but rather with which supplier can be paid the latest. Since the cash discount must be foregone, all suppliers will be paid the full amount for their merchandise. Thus the supplier that can be paid the latest is preferable. In this case supplier B will be selected, since it can be paid on day 70, later than any of the other suppliers.

Case 3: If the Tee and Tee Company already has sufficient short term financing, from which supplier should it make the purchase?

In this case the firm will take the cash discount, so the cost of foregoing it is not relevant. The chief consideration is who can be paid the least the latest. It is advisable for the firm to make its purchase from supplier D.

The effects of stretching accounts payable: -

If a firm anticipants stretching accounts payable, the cost of foregoing a cash discount is reduced. Stretching accounts payable is, sometimes suggested as a reasonable strategy for a firm if its credit rating is not damaged. Illustration: -

The Tee and Tee Company, discussed earlier, was extended credit terms of 2/10 net 30 EOM. The cost of foregoing the cash discount, assuming payment on the last day of the credit period, was found to be approximately 36 percent (2% / 20) x 360. If the firm were able to stretch its account payable to 70 days without damaging its credit rating, the cost of foregoing the cash discount would be only 12 percent (2% /60) x 360. Stretching accounts payable reduces the implicit cost of foregoing a cash discount. The length of the firm can stretch its accounts payable without damage to its credit rating must be kept in mind in evaluating the firm's cash discount strategy.

Advantages of Trade Credits

- Easily available

- It is flexible without restriction

- It requires no collateral

- It is not expensive than overdraft

iii. Accruals and Deferral Income

These are liabilities for the services received whose payments are yet to be effected. The most common items accrued by a company are taxes, wages, and proposed dividends. Deferral income is advance payment received by the company from its customers before the services are rendered or goods are supplied.

The use of accruals as ana interest-free source of financing is consistent with the general philosophy of paying bills as late as possible if the firm does not damage its credit standing. In the case of accrued wages, the firm must be careful not to dampen the morale of its employees by delaying the payment of wages for too long.

OTHERS NOTABLE SOURCE INCLUDES:

1. Business loans

Business loans typically allow you to borrow an agreed sum of money and pay it back over a certain period with interest. There are two major types of loans:

Secured business loans: The borrower of the loan puts up some collateral such as a house, car, or shares against the value of the loan. If repayment fails, the asset can become forfeit to the loan provider.

Unsecured business loans: The borrower of the loan doesn't put up any collateral, the loan is given based on the borrower's current situation.

Business loans are generally seen as a source of finance for the medium to long-term. Typically, loans are advantageous as there are many options available, both commercially and government-backed (like the startup loans scheme). You're not selling equity in your business like with venture capital, and you can shop around for an affordable payment rate and plan. For companies in the UK, there are also some tax benefits on paying back a loan.

If you do take out a business loan, make sure the payment terms and timeline is realistic for your situation and gives you some room if things don't quite go to plan. Loans remain the most popular option for businesses starting out and one of the most popular finance options for companies looking to expand.

If you are applying for a loan, the primary requisite is that your finances and accounts are up to date, and you have a clear plan to pay it back. Of course, depending on the loan provider, there can be many other prerequisites such as monthly revenue, credit rating, years trading, etc.

2. Invoice finance

Invoice financing allows companies to borrow money against the value of invoices due from customers. There are two primary forms of invoice finance, being invoice factoring and discounting. Typically, you can receive up to 85% of the value straight away and the remaining amount (minus the finance charge) when the customer pays the invoice.

Invoice finance can be a great option if you have many corporate or SME customers who have long payment terms or tend to pay as late as possible. It's a great finance option for plugging holes in cashflow. Your invoice is generally bought as debt in most cases; it's common practise that if the invoice isn't paid, you will be shielded from any debt owed.

Although this is an excellent option for finance, invoice financing is only available to companies with a strong track record of generating revenue and getting paid by customers. It's designed to alleviate the problems that come from 30, 60, 90 or more day payment terms agreed with customers that can cause finance shortfalls.

If you're looking to gain invoice finance, you'll need up to date financials and accounts, and your customers will typically need to be reasonably large for anyone to finance your invoice.

3. Business overdrafts

A bank overdraft is an ideal source of finance for the short-term. An agreed overdraft lets businesses use their current account to make payments which exceed their available balance. In other words, the company owes the bank money when the balance goes below zero.

You can borrow anything up to an agreed limit, known as the facility. Companies can negotiate different amounts with the bank, depending on their need and credit history. Some banks charge an overdraft facility fee, in addition to the interest charged on the overdrawn credit. For a larger overdraft facility, banks may require companies to put up security in the form of tangible fixed assets, or a personal guarantee made by the company's director.

Overdraft financing is useful when a business struggles with timely cash flow. Overdrafts are particularly helpful to cover short-term cash flow shortages from seasonal activities. Banks tend to review overdrafts on an annual basis.

Given the high-interest rates, overdrafts should not be a permanent source of finance. Banks can revoke an overdraft at any time and demand full repayment of the owed funds. For a more permanent solution, consider a bank loan.

4. Business credit cards

Another similar source of short-term business finance is a business credit card, which is the most commonly used finance source for small businesses. Companies can use the credit card to pay for any business-related expenses and won't incur any interest, provided the outstanding balance is paid off by the end of the credit-free period, usually 30-56 days later.

If you don't pay the balance within the credit-free period, you'll accrue interest on the outstanding credit. Each card offers a different credit limit, which puts a cap on the amount you can borrow, typically up to £10,000.

A business credit card is incredibly useful for new startups as it massively increases a company's purchasing power. In the short-term, the credit is completely free. However, it can be hard to keep track of credit card spending, which can damage your credit. If you don't manage to pay off the funds owed each money, you can start racking up considerable debt with sizeable interest rates.

Using a credit card responsibly is also an excellent way to build a positive credit report for your company, which is useful for securing loan funding later down the line. While it's a fantastic source of instant finance, they should be reserved for temporary short-term use.

5. Startup loans

Entrepreneurs can make use of a startup loan to fund their new venture. This form of finance is a personal loan backed by the government, available to individuals looking to start or grow a UK-based business. Not only do successful applicants secure funding, but they also receive 12-months business mentoring, completely free.

Startup loans can offer up to £25,000 of borrowed credit for individuals starting a business. The loan has a competitive fixed interest rate per year and offers a repayment term of 1-5 years.

This source of funding is one of the most attractive available to startups, offering a considerable amount of finance, coupled with valuable expertise. You can apply on the government website provided that you're 18, based in the UK and your business has been trading for less than 24 months.

6. Merchant cash advance

Any business using a card terminal to accept payments from customers can secure merchant cash advance from lenders through their terminal provider. The terminal provider can see exactly how much money is flowing into your business, and the lenders provide funds in exchange for a percentage of the company's daily credit card income. This visibility acts as security for the loan; you'll agree on a loan amount and repayment plan based on your average monthly profit and your cash flow.

Repayments are usually made as a percentage of revenue, meaning they remain proportionate with your business' income. Such an arrangement works well for businesses without a stable income, such as seasonal businesses. As the card terminal secures the lending, there's no need for any assets to back the finance, which is perfect for many SMEs.

Generally, you're able to secure finance equivalent to your monthly revenue. If you're making £2,000 per month, expect to secure £2,000 in merchant cash funding. The repayment structure tends to have a shorter repayment term than other sources of finance, usually under 24 months, and uses regular small payments, typically paid every business day.

7. Commercial mortgage

If you're looking to grow your business, you might be looking to invest in property. Commercial mortgages enable you to secure a 70-75% mortgage lasting up to 25 years. For investments, the amount you can borrow depends on the rental income generated by the property, up to 65% of the purchase price.

Lenders consider commercial mortgages higher-risk than regular home mortgages.

The interest rate is therefore considerably higher, and aren't fixed-rate for extended periods. That said, commercial mortgages offer better interest rates than business loans. The interest on your mortgage is tax-deductible, and you can rent out the property to generate extra income to match increased interest rates.

Be aware that mortgages are a form of secured loan, meaning the property serves as collateral for the lender. If you default on your payments, you'll lose ownership. Some lenders require additional security in the form of other fixed assets. It's worth using a mortgage broker to help you find the best offer, as they'll advise you on which providers to apply to, and can help you find the highest loan to value ratio (LTV).

8. Asset finance

Asset finance is a form of financing for businesses which require capital to purchase high-value equipment or machinery, or for companies who need to release cash from assets they already own.

Asset finance for new assets comes in the form of hire purchase, a finance lease and an operating lease. Alternatively, you can use asset finance to secure lending against an existing asset, if you can't keep up with the loan payments, known as asset-backed lending.

Asset finance differs from more traditional asset-based or secured loans, in that the asset acquired by the financier is typically the security used against the loan, meaning the business does not need to provide another form of security. You can find the main types of asset finance explored below.

Hire purchase

Hire purchase (HP) is a form of asset finance where firms can acquire assets through an asset finance provider, who agrees to purchase an asset that the business needs, outright. The company then spreads the cost out over time in instalments paid to the asset finance company. Ownership is transferred to the business at the end of the leasing period, once all instalments have been paid.

Hire purchase is an excellent option if you don't have the current capital to make the purchase. It's a fixed-rate loan with low-interest rates, ideal for assets that you need long-term. You can pay a large initial payment followed by smaller amounts, making it one of the more flexible asset finance options. The payment term is usually 1-5 years, so if you only need the asset in the short-term, you should consider a less risky option, such as leasing.

At the end of the leasing period, you'll need to pay a final fee, which is a percentage of the asset's value. In accountancy terms, the asset is treated as if you own it during the lease period, meaning it will appear as an asset on your balance sheet. The hire purchase amount shows as a liability on the balance sheet, which reduces as the firm makes each HP payment. You therefore need to consider whether the asset will depreciate over time, as while your asset will have less value each year due to depreciation, your liability remains the same.

A significant disadvantage of asset finance is that you don't officially own the asset until the end of the lease-period, meaning you're unable to make any modifications to the purchase until this time has elapsed. If you need autonomy over the asset, consider other forms of finance.

9. Finance Lease

With a finance lease, the asset finance provider agrees to purchase an asset outright and lease it to the business over a fixed period. It works in a similar way to hire purchase, the key difference being that the company will never own the asset: the intention is always that the finance company will sell the asset at the end of the lease period. In some cases, the finance company may offer the business a share in the sale value of an item when they sell it.

A lease is useful for bigger assets such as land or property that you'll use over longer periods. As you don't technically own the asset, it doesn't appear on your balance sheet, which can offer some tax benefits. You can offset your rental costs as an expense against your profit, allowing you to claim VAT. However, you will have to pay for the full value over time, making it only suitable for lease over most of the asset's life.

Operating leases

Operating leases are a preferable option to lease equipment, as the lease company takes care of the maintenance. The rental agreement also includes a set term, which is useful when a business may not need an asset for its full usable life. You only pay for the value of the asset over the time of your rental agreement, which is usually cheaper than paying for the full value of the item, as with a finance lease.

As with a finance lease, the asset won't appear on your balance sheet, meaning you can offset your rent against your profit. At the end of the term, the business can either choose to renew the lease or return the asset. During the lease period, a company has full access to the asset, meaning you're responsible for insurance and maintenance costs.

Asset-based lending

Asset-based lending allows businesses to release cash from existing assets. The company sells an asset to a finance provider for an agreed amount and then pays back this lump sum in the form of a lease, making regular payments over an agreed period. The company recoups the purchase cost and interest. This form of asset finance is useful if a company cannot keep up with maintenance costs or loan payments on a valuable asset.

10. Crowdfunding

Crowdfunding has really grown as a source of investment for businesses overall and for specific products. It involves taking a small amount of investment from a lot of people to equal a much larger sum. Crowdfunding can be divided into two types:

Equity based: You give away equity in return for investment funds.

Rewards based: You give away perks, rewards or thanks for people supporting a specific product or business.

Loan based: You can crowdfund loan, hence source of finance.

High tech and product based businesses generally use crowdfunding. It's important to consider that the success of a crowdfunding campaign is typically reliant on your ability to market your proposition. It can be a great source of finance, especially if you're launching a product, as you're effectively doing pre-sales to fund development and launch. There is also a good range of crowdfunding platforms to choose from, including kickstarter, Seedrs, Crowdcube and IndieGoGo.

If you're looking to raise money to start or grow your business, equity-based crowdfunding has become a popular way to do it. Be careful though; unless there's a nominee structure, you may have to report to thousands of small shareholders if you raise funds this way.

11. Grants

Small business grants are typically awarded by the government, a government body or a charitable outside body. Grants usually take the form of finance, available to organisations or individuals that meet specific criteria and undergo an application and vetting process.

For example, Innovate UK is a government body providing grants for innovation in certain areas of the UK economy. These grants aim to help support specific businesses and sectors of the economy engaged in a particular type of research and development.

Grants can range in size from £500 to over £1 million, with the majority in the UK sitting between £3,000 and £100,000. Grants are a brilliant source of finance for businesses as they don't have to be paid back. Still, they are tough to apply for, very competitive and often only available for very specific companies or those engaged in particular areas of research.

The main consideration as to whether you apply for a grant or not should be the time it will take you to complete the application, compared to the likelihood of getting the funding, with further consideration given to what you could be doing instead of applying to raise finance.

12. Venture capital

Venture capital is a good option for high growth companies looking for serious finance in exchange for equity. Typically, VC money in the UK starts from £500K and goes up to £50 million for a single investment.

VC is a popular way for companies who are in a growth stage to raise; you'll need a business that is scalable and has evident traction to date. Also, be prepared to be seriously audited if a VC is looking to invest in you: have your books and plans up to date.

Finally, bear in mind that you're taking on a serious equity partner who has experience investing professionally. VCs bring lots of money but also pressure and structure beyond what you have currently, so make sure you're ready for that.

13. Angel investment

If you're looking to raise a small amount of finance to start out, then raising investment from angels is probably the best way to get it. Investments typically range from £10K to £500K (under SEIS or EIS). Raising from an angel is often much more straightforward than raising from VC or institutional funds.

With an angel investor, you'll also likely get a mentor and an experienced partner as an investor to support you in starting your business. Try to make sure your partner understands your area as well; experience can be more valuable than money. A media company, for example, should get an investor who has significant experience in media.

CAPITAL FORMATION:

Capital formation or accumulation plays a predominant role in all types of economics whether they are of the American or the British type, or the Chinese type. Development is not possible without capital formation. Capital formation refers to all the produced means of further production, such as roads, railways, bridges, canals, dams, factories, seeds, fertilisers, etc.

capital formation can be liken to that which society does not apply the whole of its current productive activity to the needs and desires of immediate consumption, but directs a part of it to the tools and making of capital goods: tools and instruments, machines and transport facilities, plant and equipment— all the various forms of real capital that can so greatly increase the efficacy of productive effort. The essence of the process, then, is the diversion of a part of society's currently available resources to the purpose of increasing the stock of capital goods so as to make possible an expansion of consumable output in the future."

Saving and investment are essential for capital formation. According to Marshall, saving is the result of waiting or abstinence. When a person postpones his consumption to the future, he saves his wealth which he utilizes for further production, If all people save like this, the aggregate savings increase which are utilised for investment purposes in real capital assets like machines, tools, plants, roads, canals, fertilizers, seeds, etc.

But savings are different from hoardings. For savings to be utilised for investment purposes, they must be mobilised in banks and financial institutions. And the businessmen, the entrepreneurs and the farmers invest these community savings on capital goods by taking loans from these banks and financial institutions. This is capital formation.

So, what does capital mean to businesses? Capital is anything that increases your ability to generate value. You can use capital to increase value in your business's financial assets. Generally, business capital includes financial assets held by your company that you can use to leverage growth and build financial stability.

Capital and cash are not one and the same. Capital can be stronger than cash because you can use it to produce something and generate revenue and income (e.g., investments). But because you can use capital to make money, it is considered an asset in your books (i.e., something that adds value to your business).

So, how does capital work? Companies can use capital to invest in anything to create value for their business. The more value it creates, the better the return for the business.

Capital examples

So, what does capital include? Capital can expand to a variety of things in business, both tangible and intangible. Here are a few examples of capital:

Company cars

Machinery

Patents

Software

Brand names

Bank accounts

Stocks

Bonds

There are also different types of capital in business, including:

Working capital

Use this capital to pay for day-to-day business operations

Converts into cash more quickly than other investments (e.g., a new oven at a bakery)

Debt capital

Capital a business earns from taking out loans and debt

Equity capital

Comes in several forms, including public equity and private equity (e.g., shares of stock in the company)

Trading capital

Amount of money available to a company for purchasing and selling assets

examples of trading capital in business

Capital gains and losses

When you make an investment, the goal is to generate wealth for your business to help it grow and expand. And as your investments grow your business, the capital itself can increase in value, which can result in capital gains.

Capital gains

When your capital's worth increases, you see a capital gain. A capital gain occurs when your investment is worth more than its purchase price.

For example, say you buy a machine for $1,500. The machine needs work, but you fix it without needing any new parts. You then turn around and sell it for $2,000 because you gave it a higher value by fixing it.

To calculate the gain in your business accounting records, take the final sale price of the machine ($2,000) and subtract the initial purchase price ($1,500). Your accounting records should reflect a gain of $500.

Capital losses

Not every investment is going to be worth it in the end. This is where capital losses come into play. With a capital loss, your investment is worth less than its initial purchase price.

Let's take a look at the machine example again. You purchase the machine for $1,500, but you spend $600 on new parts to fix the machine before you sell it for $2,000. Between the cost of the machine and its new parts, you spend $2,100. This is considered a capital loss of $100 because you spent more money on the total investment ($2,100) than you received for the sale ($2,000). In your books, record a capital loss of $100.

Capital in accounting

Business owners can use their capital records to make savvy investments and help make smart financial decisions. But in order to do that, your accounting records need to be as accurate as possible.

To easily track capital, make smart financial moves, and avoid major mistakes, record your investments in your books regularly. And be sure to examine them to see what's working and what isn't.

To easily track capital in your books, you can opt to use accounting software. That way, you can record your capital quickly and avoid making accounting mistakes yourself. Plus, you can access numerous reports and financial statements to help make investments and decisions.

To determine if an investment was worth it, examine your books and ask yourself the following questions:

Did the capital I invested in help grow my company?

Am I in a good place financially that I can invest more in my company?

Which investments were not worth it?

When your capital is growing, so is your business. So to keep your business prospering, build a solid strategy for tracking, using, and gaining investments.

Process of Capital Formation:

The process of capital formation involves three steps:

(1) Increase in the volume of real savings.

(2) Mobilisation of savings through financial and credit institutions; and

(3) Investment of savings.

Thus the problem of capital formation becomes two-fold: one, how to save more; and two, how to utilise the current savings of the community for capital formation. We discuss the factors on which capital accumulation depends.

1. Increasing Savings:

(a) Power and Will to Save:

Savings depend upon two factors: the power to save and the will to save. The power to save of the community depends upon the size of the average income, the size of the average family, and the standard of living of the people.

Other things being equal, if the income of the people increases, or the size of the family is small, or people get accustomed to a particular standard of living which does not lean towards conspicuous consumption, the power to save increases.

The power to save also depends upon the level of employment in the country. If employment opportunities increase, and existing techniques and resources are employed fully and efficiently, incomes increase, and so do the propensity of the people to save.

Savings also depend upon the will to save. People may themselves forego consumption in the present and save. They may do so to meet emergencies, for family purposes, or for social status. But they will save only if certain facilities or inducements are available.

People save if the government is stable and there is peace and security in the country. People do not save when there is lawlessness and disorder, and there is no security of life, property and business.

The existence of banking and financial institutions paying high rates of interest on different term-deposits also induces people to save more. The taxation policy of the government also affects the savings habits of the people.

Highly progressive income and property taxes reduce the incentive to save. But low rates of taxation with due concessions for savings in provident fund, life insurance, health insurance, etc. encourage savings.

(b) Perpetuation of Income Inequalities:

Perpetuation of income inequalities had been one of the major sources of capital formation in 18th century England and early 20th century Japan. In most communities, it is the higher income groups with a high marginal propensity to save that do the majority of savings.

If there is unequal distribution of income, the society's upper level incomes accrue to the businessmen, the traders and the landlords who save more and hence invest more on capital formation. But this policy of deliberately creating inequalities is not favoured now either in developed or developing economics when all countries aim at reducing income inequalities.

(c) Increasing Profits:

Professor Lewis is of the view that the ratio of profits to national income should be increased by expanding the capitalist sector of the economy, by providing various incentives and protecting enterprises from foreign competition. The essential point is that profits of business enterprises should increase because they know how to use them in productive investment.

(d) Government Measures:

Like private households and enterprises, the government also saves by adopting a number of fiscal and monetary measures. These measures may be in the form of a budgetary surplus through increase in taxation (mostly indirect), reduction in government expenditure, expansion of the export sector, raising money by public loans, etc.

If people are not saving voluntarily, inflation is the most effective weapon. It is regarded as hidden or invisible tax. When prices rise, they reduce consumption and thus divert resources from current consumption to investment. Besides, the government can increase savings by estab-lishing and running public undertakings more efficiently so that they earn larger profits which are utilised for capital formation.

2. Mobilisation of Savings:

The next step for capital formation is the mobilisation of savings through banks, investment trusts, deposit societies, insurance companies, and capital markets. "The kernal of Keynes's theory is that decisions to save and decisions to invest are made largely by different people and for different reasons." To bring the savers and investors together there must be well-developed capital and money markets in the country.

In order to mobilise savings, attention should be paid to the starting of investment trusts, life insurance, provident fund, banks, and cooperative societies. Such agencies will not only permit small amounts of savings to be handled and invested conveniently but will allow the owners of savings to retain liquidity individually but finance long-term investment collectively.

3. Investment of Savings:

The third step in the process of capital formation is the investment of savings in creating real assets. The profit-making classes are an important source of capital formation in the agricultural and industrial sectors of a country.

They have an ambition for power and save in the form of distributed and undistributed profits and thus invest in productive enterprises, besides, there must be a regular supply of entrepreneurs which are capable, honest and dependable.

To perform his economic function, the entrepreneur requires two things, according to Professor Schumpeter, first, the existence of technical knowledge to produce new products; second, the power of disposal over the factors of production in the form of bank credit.

To these may he added, the existence of such infrastructure as well-developed means of transport, communications, power, water, educated and trained personnel, etc. Further, the social, political and economic climatic conditions in the country must be conducive for the emergence of a growing supply of entrepreneurs.

Domestic sources for capital formation are required to be supplemented by external sources. There are two reasons for external borrowing, according to Professor A.J. Brown. One is that it may be the easiest way of getting hold of capital funds at all, and the other that it may be the easiest way of getting foreign currency with which to buy imports which are needed for development.

The countries which have borrowed most from abroad for development purposes are those which have at some stage had a colonial status, have been developed by European immigrants, or have traded heavily with the highly developed countries, or have satisfied all these conditions.

For instance, the United States, in spite of its high rate of internal saving was a heavy foreign borrower in the earlier part of its development, with a net foreign indebtedness which in the eighteen-nineties perhaps reached 4 or 5 per cent of its already very large capital.

Capital Formation in a Socialist Economy:

The above description is of the process of capital formation in a capitalist economy. In a socialist economy, capital formation is entirely done by the state. Since all capital and land is owned by the state and all products are produced by it, all rent, interest and profits are received by the state which invests them for creating capital assets.

The state fixes the rate of capital formation to be achieved for each year and takes away a part of the income of the people through fixation of higher prices for products and taxation. In a socialist state, savings are done on a much larger scale by the state than in a capitalist economy.

It is the government which saves out of the proceeds of taxation, and profits of enterprises. The main source is the turnover tax on consumers' goods. Then there are the profit-margins, as the difference between the prices of consumers' goods fixed and their costs of production.

After allowing some percentage of these profit-margins to enterprises for approved capital purposes, the rest are allocated for investment purposes along with the revenue from the turnover tax. Personal savings lying in banks or subscribed to state loans also account for about 15 to 20 per cent of the total savings which are utilised for capital formation in a socialist economy.

MANAGEMENT OF FINANCIAL RESOURCE

Financial Resource are those resources acquired through the owners' contributions, creditors, sales of company's products and other sources. The resources ae committed, by the management into various assets to achieve the goals and objectives of the company.

The management and control of financial resources is of vital importance to companies and forms a major workload function of the finance and accountant.

Effective financial management is vital for business survival and growth. It involves planning, organising, controlling and monitoring your financial resources in order to achieve your business objectives.

Good financial management will help your business to make effective use of resources, fulfil commitments to your stakeholders, gain competitive advantage and prepare for long-term financial stability.

Financial management should become part of the key processes within your business and be included in your ongoing planning.

You might feel that your finances are complicated and confusing but the following ten top tips should help you to gain control of them.

1. Have a clear business plan

A business plan will establish where you are and where you want to get to over the next few years. It should detail how you will finance your business and its activities, what money you will need and where it will come from - see write a business plan: step-by-step.

2. Monitor your financial position

You should regularly monitor the progress of your business. On a daily basis, you should know how much money you have in the bank, how many sales you're making and your stock levels. You should also review your position against the targets set in your business plan on a monthly basis - see cashflow management.

3. Ensure customers pay you on time

Businesses can run into major problems because of late customer payments. To reduce the risk of late or non-payment, you should make your credit terms and conditions obvious from the outset. You should also quickly issue invoices that are clear and accurate. Using a computerised credit management system will help you to keep track of customers' accounts - read ensure customers pay you on time.

4. Know your day-to-day costs

Even the most profitable of companies can face difficulties if there isn't enough cash to cover day-to-day costs such as rent and wages. You should be aware of the minimum your business needs to survive and ensure you do not go below this - see how to measure cash in your business.

5. Keep up-to-date accounting records

If your accounts are not kept up-to-date, you could risk losing money by failing to keep up with late customer payments or not realising when you have to pay your suppliers. Using a good record keeping system will help you to track expenses, debts and creditors, apply for additional funding and save time and accountancy costs - see financial and management accounts.

6. Meet tax deadlines

Failing to meet deadlines for filing tax returns and payments can incur fines and interest. These are unnecessary costs that can be avoided with some forward-planning. Keeping accurate records saves your business time and money and you can be confident that you're only paying the tax you owe. Therefore, it's important that you meet your obligations - see set up a basic record-keeping system.

7. Become more efficient and control overheads

Is your business operating at its most efficient? Saving energy and therefore money can happen by implementing changes in behaviour and using existing equipment more efficiently. It's one of the easiest ways to cut costs. Areas to look at in an average office include heating, lighting, office equipment and air conditioning - see save money by using energy more efficiently.

8. Control stock

Efficient stock control ensures you have the right amount of stock available at the right time so that your capital is not tied up unnecessarily. You should put systems in place to keep track of stock levels - taking control of this will allow you to free up cash, while also having the right amount of stock available - see common business mistakes: poor stock control.

9. Get the right funding

It is essential that you choose the right type of finance for your business - each type of finance is designed to meet different needs. Smaller businesses usually rely more on business overdrafts and personal funding but this might not be the best kind of funding for your company - read business financing options - an overview.

10. Tackle problems when they arise

It is always very stressful facing financial problems as a business, but there is help and advice available to help you tackle them before it gets too much to handle so seek professional advice as soon as possible. There are also some initial steps you can take to minimise the impact such as tackling priority debts first and assessing how you can improve your cashflow management

www.ingramcontent.com/pod-product-compliance
Lightning Source LLC
Chambersburg PA
CBHW071523220526
45472CB00003B/1133